Never Lose Your Mind Over A Woman

By: Aaron Fields

ISBN: 978-1-953962-07-2

CONTENTS

<u>Something To Think About Before You Read</u>

"As a man, there is no human being in this world that is worth the subjugation of your heart, spirit, and peace of mind."

----------Aaron Fields

Word From The Author

It's important for men to understand that in life, you are going to make mistakes. Most of the mistakes you make that will have the greatest impact will involve a woman. Most of the problems men find themselves in are because of their susceptibility to women. Therefore, the men are at fault because it's their job to understand the nature of women. A man must remain steadfast and not be fooled by the woman's stratagems, and should not conform to her belief system.

Sadly, many of these women are hurt, broken, and unstable. Keep in mind that certain women you decide to deal with can be a lustful thinker towards other men and even other women. Certain women feel the need to display and promote themselves sexually in order to receive validation from society. As a man, it is not your job to beg and seek validation from this society. It's unfortunate that some men with limited thinking feel the need to compromise themselves mentally, financially, and spiritually to seek validation from women. Gentlemen, no matter how much you try to explain it away, getting yourself worked up over a woman is not worth it. I promise you when the woman breaks up with you; she's actually doing you a favor.

It's plain to see that a majority of men in this society struggle with knowing how to move on from a breakup. To lessen the pain of a breakup, it's important not to obsess over a woman and make her an idol. If you're still struggling to get over the woman who hurt you, that's a sign you need to spend more time alone to work on yourself. Consider meditating, praying, reading the bible and studying the scriptures. If the bible doesn't captivate you, read a book that's unique to you, exercise, learn a musical instrument, or find a new hobby. As a collective, men should concentrate their brains on loftier matters that will bring joy, efficiency, and creativity. Be grateful that you don't need to experience the awful treatment from the woman you once dated, since she is someone else's burden now. Spending your life trying to win back someone who won't be won back is pointless.

Self-love must come first before you can love anyone else. Take care of yourself and always be conscious of the women you let into your life. Understand that this society is not working effectively. The interaction between men and women in this current society is extremely toxic. Gentlemen, I cannot stress this enough that losing your sanity over a woman is not worth it. If you're not prudent, your obsession with the woman could cost you your life.

1

IS IT WORTH IT?

Men, if you find yourself in a precarious situation with a female that could cause the ruination of your future and career; is throwing it all away really worth it. Losing your mind over a woman will never lead to a healthy outcome. Don't let your situation get out of control to the extent that you contemplate violence against her, her family, her property, or even yourself. It'll be best for you to just leave the relationship and move on with your life.

Believe it or not, there are a lot of replacements for the woman you are currently with. As a man, it's vital to focus your thoughts on what really matters in life, like your mission and your spiritual bond with God. If there is a woman that is coming into your life to create chaos, leave the relationship before things get worse for you.

As a man, it is your duty to ensure that your life is healthy and secure. Why? Well, it's because you never want to bring any negativity or instability into the life of others, including the woman you're with. These women have already been through a lot and are fragile, so it would be foolish on your part as a man to make matters worse. Even if she doesn't admit it, she needs you to be secure in all areas of your life (financially, mentally, emotionally, physically, and spiritually). Why? She wants to feel secure and safe. An invaluable companion in a relationship with a wonderful woman can be obtained by providing her with stability and comfort.

DON'T CRY OVER HER

There is nothing wrong with crying if someone close to you passes away or someone you love got hurt. It's not emasculating when a man sheds a few tears. However, don't waste tears on someone who brought nothing positive into your life. Also, refrain from publicizing your circumstances if possible. Right now, social media is prevalent and everyone is eager to broadcast their lives online. Once again, there is nothing wrong with a man crying because of the issues he's experiencing in his life. However, crying and complaining about women, especially over the internet is not a good look. Are you looking for sympathy? Are you looking for attention? If this is true, then you can't be surprised when society mocks you. Expect no compassion from your adversaries.

Why would you shed tears for someone you should have never taken seriously? Gentlemen, just because a woman is quick to offer you sex, that doesn't mean you should take her seriously. Just because she says she is nice, respectful, and supportive, that doesn't mean she's telling the truth. Why is that? It's because the woman has to prove her worth to you over an extended period. Keep in mind that as she shows her worth to you, it's your job to prove your worth as well by making the correct choices in all aspects of your life.

If a woman contacts you to let you know she isn't interested in continuing the relationship, that's perfectly alright. When a woman ends a relationship with you, it's actually helping you out. When a woman doesn't want to be with you anymore, it means that you have to either improve yourself as a man or it could mean that the woman was just never worth your time. Either way, it turns out to be a blessing for you.

___

DID YOU "FALL IN LOVE?"

Most men lose their mind over women because many of them are "falling in love". Understand that falling in love with your woman and loving your woman are two totally different things. Loving someone involves having the desire to see them grow, prosper, and potentially build something special with that person. However, falling in love can stem from being obsessive and overly infatuated with the other person. It makes no sense for a man to become overly infatuated with something or someone that isn't permanent.

When a man falls in love, he ends up compromising himself mentally, emotionally, financially, and spiritually. As a result, it makes it easier for him to get manipulated and controlled by the women he allows into his life. If you're a man wanting to achieve higher things in life, you cannot let this happen to you. Be careful of the people you bring into your inner circle because some of them are not concerned with your happiness. In most cases, the world will try to harm you by using the people closest to you.

If you're a man planning to achieve great things, understand that you will experience pain and distress sometimes. When a woman comes into your life, remain alert because she may not have good intentions. Any man of wisdom and knowledge will probably tell you they have had to deal with a woman that was trying to keep them from achieving their purpose. When people turn against you, remember that you're being tested and you must use good judgement and stay vigilant.

4

WHAT A YOUNG MAN MUST UNDERSTAND

Someone wise once told me that your thirties bring greater insight into the meaningful aspects of your life. So for those of you that are teenagers or in your twenties, please understand that you do not have life figured out yet. As it pertains to your interactions with women, please take your time and don't rush into a relationship that you're unsure about. I strongly suggest that if you don't have your life in order yet, you should not be looking at getting women pregnant or getting married. If you're interacting with a woman, take the time to understand her mindset and watch how she conducts herself and responds to adversity.

When the woman in your life suddenly creates chaos and makes things harder for you, don't let it get to a point when you develop homicidal or suicidal thoughts. It's not healthy, and it's not wise. Again, it's important for you to understand the difference between loving her and falling in love with her. Once you're able to grasp those two concepts, you'll develop a different perspective.

Another important concept that you young men must understand is the difference between a low-quality woman and a high-quality woman. Just because the woman is so quick to give herself up sexually for you, doesn't mean you should make her your wife or girlfriend. Who knows? Maybe the woman doesn't really want to be with you, and if that's true, then let her go so you can move on. You can't be too concerned with how these women think because most of them don't even care what you think. That's why it's important for you young men to vet and evaluate the women you deal with. Once again, take your time with them because if the woman you are currently with is worth making her your girlfriend or your wife, she'll show it to you in due time.

VERIFY YOUR OPTIONS

As a man, there is nothing wrong with weighing your options. If you feel the need to date more than one woman until you get a better idea of the woman you want, then do what you have to do. As long as you're honest, careful, respectful of them, and aware of the situation you're in. Remember to always keep things in its proper perspective and continue to focus on your purpose in life because some women will try to impede that.

While you're verifying your options, never let society shame you into believing that you have no morals or character. Your reputation as a man of integrity should not be in jeopardy just because you want to take your time in getting to know the woman more efficiently. If the woman doesn't like the way how you're doing things, make it clear to her that she has the power to end the relationship whenever she chooses. As I mentioned earlier, if the woman is worth being exclusive with, she'll prove herself to you as time goes on.

A huge part in verifying your options as a man is to understand how a woman operates. Even though it's essential to show love and affection to your woman, it's also crucial to keep your primary focus on God. In addition to that, you want to make sure you can to be a positive member of society. Once again, gentlemen, verify your options first before you get with someone that will cause you to get off track.

In case you haven't realized this yet, it's not normal to go back and forth with the woman all the time. If she's always trying to argue with you, that is a major red flag. A genuine woman is not trying to argue all the time. If you're a man that is healthy and stable in every aspect of your life, there shouldn't be that many reasons for a woman to start an argument with you. If you're a man and your woman is picking a fight despite you doing everything the right way, it could be a sign that she wants to end the relationship. Or it's possible that she doesn't feel worthy of being with you, but either way, that's okay. Move on with your life and consider your options because you don't want to be with someone that will one day sabotage you.

6

WHAT IF SHE WRONGS ME?

Gentlemen, if a woman cheats on you, or breaks up with you, don't go off your rocker. Why? It's because you never want to give a woman the satisfaction of knowing that she has the power to alter your emotional state anytime she wants. Women are wonderful and beautiful human beings, but a lot of you guys have an unhealthy obsession with them. Parting ways with a woman who has been negative throughout the relationship should make you feel happy. Always learn from other men's mistakes. Also, never try to win back your ex by crying, attempting suicide, or posting embarrassing messages on social media. It's important that you develop some respect for yourself. It's important for men to understand that no means no. If a woman decides she's no longer interested in being with you, it's important to respect her decision and move on with your life.

Most of you guys are struggling to move on with your life, partly because you keep thinking about the next man that she's currently intimate with. You must get over it and let it go because the next guy that deals with her is going to be his problem now, not yours. When you're too attached or hooked on a woman, you risk getting manipulated and damaged. That's why falling in love is not healthy and fruitful for you.

Don't allow your feelings to overpower you if a woman mistreats you, especially if she knows everything about you. That's why you must be careful of the type of women you're vulnerable with. There is nothing wrong with being vulnerable with someone trustworthy. You need to be cautious when exposing your weakness to a toxic woman, because she will use it to her advantage and exploit you. To overcome this, you must start off by acknowledging your weakness. Remember, there is nothing wrong with a man acknowledging his weakness because that means he's on the path to becoming a better person.

It's inevitable that bad things are going to happen to you. When there's a chink in your armor, all you need to do is repair it. You always want to learn and grow from your mistakes so you can become a better man. Above all else, if you have conquered your challenges, I would like to motivate you to teach and guide other men on how to achieve the same. Many men have avoided suicide because of helpful information from a father, a program, a YouTube video, or even a book. Fortunately, many of you guys can now read a certain book or watch a certain YouTube video that will help restore and revitalize your spirit. Since we have access to a ton of information, there should be no excuses for killing yourself over a woman. I have news for you; there will never be a woman on this planet worth killing yourself over. I don't care how pretty her face is or how great her body is. Going through all that trouble for any woman isn't worth it.

What would you do if a woman cheats on you? What would you do if you suddenly received a text message saying "I don't want to be with you anymore"? How would you respond to that? What will you do?

_____

_____

_____

_____

_____

_____

_____

_____

_____

_____

_____

_____

_____

_____

_____

_____

_____

_____

7

TRY PUTTING GOD FIRST

Another reason many of you are losing your mind over these women is because you lost your connection with God. One of the most important things to have as a man is a strong spiritual connection with God. It's also important that you learn how to embrace solitude. Trust me, this will help you maintain your sanity and create a healthy balance in your life.

Achieving a balanced life is important so you don't become so dependent on something or someone that your life revolves around it. That is what you call idolatry, and you cannot have that in your life. When you idolize women, you bring in chaos and confusion.

Before you get into a serious relationship with a woman, I challenge you to imagine what your life would be like if she betrayed you, even if it never happens. How would you react? What would you do? How would you live? These are the questions you have to think about and hopefully these bad things won't happen to you. You always have to hope for the best, and prepare for the worse. Sometimes you just never know because a lot of women are very fickle minded.

When you put the woman before God, life is going to stop you from developing into a productive man in this society. You must be prepared for anything when it comes to women, since they are unpredictable. Now, does this mean you should hate women? No, it just means you have to understand women's nature and how they operate.

From a biblical perspective, the fall of man started once Adam put Eve over God. The reason Adam suffered wasn't because he didn't understand God. It was because he understood the laws of God, but he still put Eve on a pedestal. Understand that God will be the only consistent thing in your life, not the woman. Many of you guys don't understand this concept and once the woman takes you to court, cheats on you, or breaks up with you, then suddenly you hate women. Your feelings towards the woman are not just of hatred, but you also have hatred for yourself for not being able to comprehend her. Once you get a better understanding of women, you won't have time to hate them. It's very important that you understand the value of your manhood. Men have been their own worst enemy throughout history because of their obsession with women.

8

PROTECT YOURSELF

Your mind and spirit are the only things that will protect you when dealing with women. Your mind and spirit will give you power, strength, love, and self-control. Keep in mind, it takes many years to get to know a woman and what she's capable of doing to you. It's typical for women to keep certain aspects of their lives and backgrounds hidden, including their dual personalities. Why do they do this? They know that if the man finds out who they really are, they won't be able to deceive him.

Once you guys understand the nature of women, you will know how to handle them. It's like an adult going into the pet store to get a puppy. Before you bring a puppy into your home, you have to understand the responsibilities that come with getting a pet. You also have to love and understand the nature of that puppy in order for the two of you to function properly. This same concept applies to the women you deal with. As a man, can you give her knowledge and wisdom? Are you willing to exercise forgiveness and patience with her? Do you have the capacity to provide her with love and affection? If you're not able to manage these matters, then the relationship won't be sustainable. That's why it's important for the man to establish the rules of engagement and exercise patience with the woman.

Gentlemen, in case you haven't noticed this by now, the woman is playing games with not only you, but with herself. Most of these women view men like candy at a candy store, and every person of interest that they encounter is like a new piece of candy. Over time, they become tired of the same candy because they're looking for something new. Once they take an interest in the new candy, you will observe a shift in their attitude, demeanor, and outlook towards the old candy. That's why it's necessary to get mentally prepared and accept this as a potential outcome. By using this approach, you won't be as angry or depressed if a woman mistreats you.

As long as you protect your mind and spirit, you won't get caught up in many of these situations. It is essential that you grasp the woman's character, as well as your own responsibilities, especially when entering a relationship. Unfortunately, stories about men engaging in violence and self-destruction in relationships are too common in the news. Rather than idolizing women and losing your composure over them, concentrate on cultivating a tranquil state of mind.

Activity: Name at least three things in your life that will give you a peace of mind (other than being with a woman). After writing your three things down, meditate on your answers and think of ways on how you can gain that peace of mind again.

1. _____

_____

_____

9

WHY IS THE WOMAN CONFUSING TO YOU?

The confusion men experience when it comes to women is partly due to the different values society teaches women. There is a belief in this society that women should not devote themselves to a man, which may account for why there are so many of them not in healthy relationships. Perhaps society is partially to blame for the toxic dynamic between men and women. Could it be possible that men lack stability and maturity in certain aspects of their lives, besides societal influence? Maybe this is the reason men don't get any respect from women. As the result of the man's inability to function, he won't develop the knowledge, or the ability to maintain self-control. When you have no self-control as a man, you lack the understanding of your own spirit to balance out the woman's energy.

In order to interact with a woman successfully, a man has to have peace, structure, and a level of calmness in his spirit. Before engaging in serious conversations with women, having your life in order is important. If you don't have your life in order, it can be quite challenging to maintain a balance between your life and the woman's.

Don't allow her craziness to make you go crazy. Losing your mind over a woman is nothing but a manifestation of your weakness as a man. Gentlemen, do not allow your situation with the woman to stress you out. Otherwise, you'll end up making a regretful decision. If the woman is not bringing any peace into your life, just leave. Most men are damaged by women. They have wonderful experiences with the women in the beginning, only to find out that the women are not interested in staying in the relationship. When some of these women get bored, they will change up on you. If that happens, are you courageous enough to step away from the toxicity and prioritize your own happiness?

It may not be encouraging, but if you meet a woman who is not compatible with you, consider that the relationship may not be successful. Now, I wouldn't suggest that you say this to the woman directly to her. However, you should at least have that understanding in the back of your mind and know that it's okay if the woman doesn't want to be with you. The woman's choices will determine how much longer the relationship will last. If the woman you're with suddenly stops treating you with the same kindness and respect as before, it's her way of telling you it's time to move on.

Challenge Activity: In this activity, write one or multiple difficult things that you've experienced with a woman. However, while you're writing, I challenge you to not write anything bad or negative about the woman. Focus more on the grueling experience you had and what you learned from it. The goal is for you to use your experiences as something useful and empowering instead of something to stress you out.

_____

_____

_____

_____

_____

_____

_____

_____

_____

_____

_____

_____

_____

_____

_____

_____

_____

YOUR LIFE CAN'T BE ABOUT THE WOMAN

I believe it's important for a man to take on a specific interest that is spiritually based or something that is manifested into something great for his life. Why am I saying this? It's because your life should never revolve around women. For you guys that ingratiate yourself with women, enjoy the ride because things are not always guaranteed to last. If it's time for the relationship to end, exit stage left. There was a man who dealt with her before you, and there's going to be another man who will deal with her after you.

As a man, you shouldn't make your life about her, especially when you have other things to focus on. If you are married and have children with her, naturally your life involves them because they are a top priority. Hopefully, your relationship with them is beneficial and will last for a long time. It is important to love, cherish, honor and respect the woman, but you must be mindful and tread carefully because of her nature.

When men meet women, they instantly become infatuated and think the relationship will be everlasting. Understand that some women are not thinking on that level. She's more so thinking about how much fun she's going to have with you at that very moment. Don't get angry and upset when the woman shows you her true colors. Consider it to be a blessing. That's why men need to focus on the things that actually matter in life. There is never a reason to kill a woman and/or yourself over a silly relationship. Life is already challenging and stressful, so go out, enjoy yourself and make the most of the time you have left on this earth.

DON'T STORE YOUR ANGER

Over the years, I've seen so many men build up so much anger and resentment towards women because things didn't turn out well in the relationship. Gentlemen, if you keep all of that negative energy inside of you, it's going to come out in the most terrifying and inconvenient way. If you're not careful, you're going to end up harming the woman, yourself, your children, or even a random person. It's hard to believe, but some of the male-on-male violence we're seeing is related to issues the men have with women.

You never want to be the guy that takes your anger out on someone else because of the issues you have going on in your personal life. Never keep that anger and resentment inside of you. Let it go, because if the woman is not treating you right, all you have to do is leave. You can either find someone else or be by yourself for a while. Keep in mind, there is nothing wrong with embracing solitude. It's essential to understand what your standards need to be in a relationship before you get into another one. If you don't clearly understand your expectations, don't engage with these women. Stop speaking to them and focus on prioritizing your own growth. It's very important for a man to understand and think about who he wants to be in his life.

Use your time alone to improve in all areas of your life, so that if you decide to pursue a relationship with a woman in the future, you can be an amazing asset. Most of you lack the understanding of female nature and the wisdom to understand yourself to be ready for a relationship. In order to protect yourself from developing anger and hostility towards the woman, don't make her into an idol.

12

IF YOU'RE A WOMAN READING THIS

If you're a woman reading this book, it's important for you to know that this book is not meant to hurt or belittle women. My goal is actually to help you all out. Why is that? Many women like the romantic idea of a man falling in love with them. If you're a woman and this applies to you, be careful what you wish for. The feeling a man gets when he falls in love with a woman is comparable to being addicted to a drug. When you're addicted to a drug, you can't just quit that drug cold turkey. If you develop a strong craving for that drug, or if the man has a deep longing for the woman, he will do whatever it takes to make her stay. Even if it involves harming her. That's why it's crucial for a man to love his woman without falling in love.

Gentlemen, keep the woman in her proper perspective. To enhance your relationships with women, you must have your life in order. You must also address any negative energies the woman may be exposed to through social media, the radio, TV, music, and the work environment. If you don't take a stand on these issues, it will be easy for society to influence the woman. That's why it's important for men to develop foresight and understanding.

There is nothing wrong with loving your woman; it only becomes a problem when you worship her. Understand that the woman can be wrong too, and if she is wrong, correct her, but do it with love and respect. Always have mercy, kindness, and patience with her, but don't let her have a psychological hold on you.

Women, I have news for you; it is not the man's job to idolize you. Instead of the man glorifying you, it'll be best for the man to tell you the truth. In order to improve in every aspect of your life, you must address the truth, even if you don't want to hear it. A woman won't benefit from a man who tells her only what she wants to hear. Ladies, if you want to be with a man who can solve problems, you can't be with someone who is always seeking your approval.

13

MESSAGE TO THE MALE MAN

Strive to be the best man you can be. Understand that we are not perfect because we all make mistakes in life. Anything that you go through in life is a learning experience. Don't spend too much time reflecting on the past. Instead, focus on what is coming. Don't let a woman drive you to the point of humiliation or unmanliness, no matter what the situation is. Even more vital, please don't embarrass yourself on social media by pleading and searching for pity, because that won't do you any good.

Just because the television says the woman is perfect, beyond criticism, and a God, doesn't mean it's true. The woman is not God; however, she is beautiful, exceptional, and essential to the world. Unfortunately, a great number of women have severe issues that need to be resolved. That's why it's important for you as the man to bring no negativity and instability into the woman's life. Make sure you know what you're doing and make sure you know exactly what you're getting yourself into. Remember to always hope for the best and prepare for the worse.

Like I said earlier, when the woman breaks up with you, she's doing you a favor. If she's more concerned with messing around with other people or worshipping herself, leave the relationship. That way, you can focus on yourself. As a grown man, embrace the idea of being by yourself. If I'm being honest, in order to achieve high levels of success in your life, you have to be secluded. You can never be successful as a man if you don't know how to be on your own. Before you start a serious relationship with a woman, work on yourself, live by yourself, and continue to focus on higher things in your life because women will take up a lot of your time. If you're not careful, some of these women will also try to test you by playing games with your sanity, because they have childish tendencies and want to see you snap. Does this apply to all women? No, it does not.

Be wary of certain tactics women will use to get you to conform to their ideologies. Don't put yourself in a position with a woman that will cause you to kowtow to her demands. If you are going to obey something, at least obey the laws of God or anything spiritually connected to the Bible. If the woman really loves and respects your beliefs, she'll understand and won't try to change you. Not all but a lot of women will try to get you to change your identity, values, and principles, mainly because they want to see if they can get you to change. What makes most of these women childish is that they love testing out the boundaries and they want to see how far they can go before there is any pushback from you. As the man, if you say nothing to her, she's going to keep going, which is why you have to set boundaries by letting her know what you will not tolerate. If she doesn't want to listen, then all you have to do is leave the relationship. If most men understood that concept, most of you wouldn't be having these kinds of issues. Don't waste your time trying to change the woman because the only person you can change is yourself. Also, always remember to put priorities first because I promise you the woman is putting herself first. Finally, always look at the red flags when dealing with women. I'm not saying she has to be perfect because men are not perfect as well. You should know that many of these women come with a great deal of baggage, whether it's psychological, emotional, physical or spiritual. Although it's not your responsibility to take ownership of her past issues, it's crucial to be aware of the problems she brings into your life.

Most of you guys have toxic rapports with women. If you think with your brain and not your genitals, most of your issues with women will go away. Always remember that none of us are perfect. As men, we've all experienced a moment of weakness at least once during our lifetime. That's why it's important that we learn and grow from our experiences and observations.

If a woman does not want to be with you anymore, take the rejection as a teachable moment and move on to a higher level of existence. Sometimes it's best to walk away from a situation for a better life outcome. Never go back and forth with people who don't want you around. If someone doesn't want you around, then that means you shouldn't be around them. When you deal with any type of rejection, it should galvanize you to elevate your life. As a man, always remember that when dealing with women, you are placeable. If a man can offer love, financial support, emotional availability, and wisdom to a woman, he will be hard to replace. If the woman leaves you even when you have everything in order, then it's her choice. In fact, when the woman leaves you, that's only going to give you more time to focus on becoming a better version of yourself. Gentlemen, it's important that you develop this mentality. Instead of getting devastated and depressed over a woman not wanting to be with you anymore, just view it as another stumbling block to overcome. The most important thing you can do as a man is to remain vigilant. Focus on loving the woman with your brain and not your genitals. More importantly, put God and other spiritual practices first in your life because that's what's going to prevent you from becoming mentally unstable and losing your mind over a woman.

Notes

www.ingramcontent.com/pod-product-compliance
Lightning Source LLC
Chambersburg PA
CBHW081528040426
42447CB00013B/3383

* 9 7 8 1 9 5 3 9 6 2 0 7 2 *